Reptiles

SIMON & SCHUSTER BOOKS FOR YOUNG READERS
An imprint of Simon & Schuster Children's Publishing Division
1230 Avenue of the Americas, New York, New York 10020

Conceived and produced by Weldon Owen Pty Ltd
59-61 Victoria Street, McMahons Point
Sydney, NSW 2060, Australia

Copyright © 2008 Weldon Owen Pty Ltd
Originally published in the U.K. by Templar Publishing
First U.S. edition 2011

WELDON OWEN PTY LTD
Managing Director Kay Scarlett
Publisher Corinne Roberts
Creative Director Sue Burk
Production Director Todd Rechner
Images Manager Trucie Henderson

Concept Development John Bull, The Book Design Company
Senior Editor Barbara Sheppard
Designer Abi Cherokee
Illustrators The Art Agency (Barry Croucher, Gary Hanna, Terry Pastor, Mick Posen,
Peter Scott), Christer Eriksson

Color reproduction by Chroma Graphics (Overseas) Pte Ltd
Printed by Toppan Leefung Printing Ltd
Manufactured in China / 0511 WON

A WELDON OWEN PRODUCTION

SIMON & SCHUSTER BOOKS FOR YOUNG READERS is a trademark of Simon & Schuster, Inc.
The text for this book is set in Meta and Rotis Serif.
10 9 8 7 6 5 4 3 2 1
Library of Congress Control Number: 2010942718
ISBN 978-1-4424-3276-5

Reptiles

Mark Hutchinson

Simon & Schuster Books for Young Readers
New York London Toronto Sydney

Contents

introducing

in *focus*

introducing

Power jump

Cuban crocodiles are able to attack prey by launching their body vertically out of the water, using only their mighty tail. Crocodiles are some of the largest and most dangerous reptiles on Earth.

What Is a…

Reptile?

Reptiles are air-breathing animals with scaly skin over a bony internal skeleton. Other animals have a skeleton and breathe air, but they have different skin: Mammals have fur or hair; birds have feathers; and amphibians have soft, often slimy skin. Unlike mammals and birds that get energy from their food, reptiles get their warmth from the Sun. Reptiles were the first animals to have waterproof, shelled eggs that protect developing babies from drying out. All reptiles thrive where the weather is warm. They can be found in environments ranging from tropical seas to freshwater ponds, from deserts and mountains to the Arctic Circle.

OFFSHOOT SPECIES

Spiny backs

Named after the scaly crest along their back, tuataras have changed little in 240 million years. They look like lizards, but they are the survivors of a separate reptile group. Almost all became extinct long before the dinosaurs died, but two kinds survive in New Zealand.

Tunnel dwellers

All 140 amphisbaenian species, known as worm lizards, spend most of their life underground. Three out of four families are limbless and use their head to burrow tunnels. The exception is the Mexican worm lizard that digs with its clawed front limbs.

Gallery of reptiles

More than 8,800 species of reptiles are alive today. New species are discovered every year. Four main branches of the reptile family tree survive: crocodiles, alligators, caimans, and gharials; lizards and snakes; turtles and tortoises; and lizardlike tuataras.

Slender snakes

Climbing species like this Amazon tree boa tightly coil the rear part of their body around a branch, leaving the front part free to grab prey.

Surprising pose

Lizards often use defense tactics to avoid being eaten. Bearded dragons open their mouth wide and expand skin under the throat to appear larger.

Attached shell

Turtles and tortoises are the only reptiles with bony shells. Turtles that live in and around water, such as Rio Grande sliders, have clawed feet and webbing between the toes.

When Reptiles
Ruled

About 315 million years ago (mya), reptiles evolved from early amphibians—the first vertebrates to make the transition from water to land. The development of eggs with a waterproof shell was the key to the reptiles' success on land. Reptiles, including dinosaurs, dominated the sky, seas, and land from 250 to 65 mya. A catastrophic event 65 mya wiped out not only the dinosaurs but other reptile groups as well. Extinct reptile groups include the dinosaurs, flying pterosaurs, and swimming plesiosaurs and ichthyosaurs. Some reptile groups survived the mass extinction, and their descendants evolved into the thousands of different reptile species alive today.

First bird *Although* Archaeopteryx *was the original link between dinosaurs and birds, this feathered animal was a weak flyer and spent much of its time on the ground. It was slightly larger than a modern pigeon, with a long, bony tail.*

Pack formation Hypsilophodon *was a runner with a light build that traveled in groups for safety. This herbivore, one of the bird-hipped dinosaurs, was a ground dweller. It was 6.5 feet (2 m) long.*

Wing bones *This reptile was the first vertebrate to fly. An elongated fourth finger bone supported the skin on its batlike wings.*

MEET THE ANCESTORS

Fossils provide valuable information about the origins of living reptile species. Scientists study fossils and compare them with live animals. From fossil evidence, scientists know that small lizardlike reptiles, such as *Hylonomus*, evolved from amphibians.

First lizard: *Ardeosaurus*
Dating back 150 mya, this reptile was one of the most complete lizard fossils found.

Earliest reptile: *Hylonomus*
Fossils of this 8-inch (20-cm) reptile, dating 315 mya, were trapped in fossilized trees.

First turtle: *Proganochelys*
Although it dates back 210 mya, the earliest known turtle has much in common with today's turtles.

First crocodile: *Protosuchus*
The first crocodile, which lived 145 mya, was about 3.3 feet (1 m) long. It had strong jaws and a powerful tail.

Trouble in paradise

Dinosaurs and other reptiles fought for survival on a European beach in the late Jurassic, about 150 mya. Early lizards ate small creatures such as insects; flying and swimming reptiles fed on small land and sea animals; and fierce predators, such as *Eustreptospondylus*, hunted other dinosaurs.

Quick escape *Fast-moving lizards, such as* Eichstaettisaurus, *easily scurried away from large predators.*

In the sea *Giant marine reptiles thrived in fish-rich tropical oceans. Dolphinlike ichthyosaurs (below) and long-necked plesiosaurs (left) share a similar ancestry.*

Hairy flyer *Like other pterosaurs,* Pterodactylus grandis *preyed on fish and small animals. Its body was covered in fine hair and it had a wingspan of about 6.5 feet (2 m).*

Jaws of death *Bladelike teeth and mighty hind legs made* Eustreptospondylus *a top predator. It was 23 feet (7 m) long. Carnivorous* Tyrannosaurus rex *was one of its descendants.*

Powerful Predators
Crocodilians

There are a total of 23 crocodilian species: two kinds of alligators, six caimans, two gharials, and 13 crocodiles. All are found in warmer parts of the world, with the exception of the endangered Chinese alligator that can survive chilly winters in partly frozen water. The enormous saltwater crocodile, the largest species, can grow to 20 feet (6 m); the smallest crocodilian, the Cuvier's dwarf caiman, is less than a quarter that size. Crocodilians are stealthy hunters that do not venture far from water. They eat insects, frogs, fish, turtles, and birds. The larger species will even feed on mammals as big as cattle and zebras.

Long distance *A female is attracted by the male alligator's vibrations. His underwater rumbling can be sensed 1 mile (1.6 km) away.*

SHAPES AND SIZES

True crocodiles have the broadest heads, and teeth that interlock and can be seen when the jaws close. Only the upper teeth of alligators and caimans are visible when the mouth is shut. Long, narrow snouts suit fish-eating gharials perfectly.

Nile crocodile
16.5 ft (5 m)

Gharial
16.5 ft (5 m)

American alligator
13 ft (4 m)

Spectacled caiman
6.5 ft (2 m)

Sound and fury

The social lives of crocodilians can be noisy. Males use sounds and actions to attract females and warn off rivals. Different species roar, blurt air through their nostrils, or slap their head down on the water. American alligators communicate by rumbling, which creates high, bubbly streams of water.

Bubbling up *The male American alligator's deep rumbling triggers powerful vibrations that send water bubbles up to 2 feet (60 cm) above the surface.*

Posturing *To make bubbles, the body is held high in the water with the head lifted and tail arched up for balance. This pose and the shimmering water make the male more noticeable to other alligators.*

Low-profile predators

Crocodilians silently glide through water, then ambush prey with a sudden rush. Their main sense organs—their eyes and ears—are located on top of the head. Only this small area needs to be above water for them to find their prey.

Crocodile tears
Upper and lower eyelids protect the eye and block light. The third eyelid wipes a lubricating fluid across the eye's surface.

Glowing eyes
A reflective layer at the back of crocodilian eyes bounces light. This layer doubles the information captured by the light-detecting cells and gives them excellent night vision.

Shut tight *Long lids covering crocodilian ears close when the animal goes underwater.*

Leaping
Lizards

There are more than 5,000 kinds of lizards, nearly two-thirds the total number of reptile species. They are classified with snakes as Squamata, "the scaly ones." Major lizard groups include geckos, skinks, anoles, wormlike amphisbaenians, chameleons, iguanas, and the ultimate lizard predators, venomous monitors and Gila monsters. Lizards eat mainly insects but can also feed on plants. Large lizards prey on other reptiles, small mammals, and birds. The Komodo dragon, the largest lizard, can kill and eat a water buffalo. Some lizards are brightly colored; others are dull and well camouflaged. Found nearly everywhere on Earth, except Antarctica, all lizards are covered with scales that prevent them from drying out in the heat and a few can hibernate over winter in burrows under the snow. Some live permanently underground.

Support system *The wings are held open by six pairs of extended ribs. When not in use, the ribs fold the wings flat against the body. Flying lizards also have skin flaps along the neck that provide extra lift and a dewlap under the chin.*

SPECIALIZED FEET

Lizard feet have evolved to suit how they move. Runners have long toes, and climbers have needle-sharp claws and sometimes Velcro-like sticky pads. Others have webbed toes or fringed scales for walking on sand or swimming.

Claspers
Chameleon feet can grasp like a human finger and thumb, but these lizards have two "thumbs" on one side.

Good grip
Gecko feet have pads covered in millions of hairlike structures that stick to most surfaces, enabling geckos to walk on ceilings.

Powerful claws
Monitor lizards have muscular limbs with thick, sharp claws for attacking prey and digging hard soil.

Whiptail
Like most lizards, the whiptail is a fast runner. Its elongated toes give it a long stride.

Soaring through the sky

Draco volans, a kind of "flying" lizard, has paper-thin flaps of skin that can stretch to form wings, like a hang glider. To escape from predators or travel between trees, the lizard leaps off a high branch, spreads its wings, and glides up to 165 feet (50 m). It can change direction midair and make a U-turn back to where it started.

Balancing act *A long tail balances the lizard's body while flying. Precise tail and wing movements help the lizard regulate speed and steer, like adjusting the rudder of a ship.*

Prepare for landing *Flying lizards spread out their sharp claws to securely grip bark when landing in a tree. Claws also help them run up tree trunks.*

Different kinds of lizards
Lizards range from Komodo dragons that can weigh more than 120 pounds (55 kg) to tiny pygmy chameleons that could sit on your finger.

Komodo dragon
10 ft (3 m)

Green iguana
6.5 ft (2 m)

Scaly-foot
18 in (45 cm)

Madagascar day gecko
9 in (22 cm)

Pygmy chameleon
1.5 in (3.5 cm)

Fierce Serpents
Snakes

Snakes have a slender body without limbs, piercing fangs, and in some, lethal venom—a great combination for stealth killers. Many of the 3,100 kinds of snakes are venomous, but fewer than a hundred species could kill a person. All snakes are carnivores, and their specialized jaws enable them to swallow prey much larger than their head. Snakes range in size from a tiny thread snake that is no bigger than a pencil to a reticulated python, the world's longest snake, reported to reach 33 feet (10 m). Found everywhere but the highest and coldest places on Earth, snakes are best suited for the warm tropics. Some have adapted to live only in the sea.

Thin end *Lacking ribs, snake tails are flexible, yet still strong. Tree climbers use their tails to grasp branches.*

See-through snake
This X-ray view reveals a skeleton that protects a rhinoceros viper's organs. Snakes usually have 150–250 vertebrae in their backbone, and long species may have 500. They have similar organs to humans, including lungs, liver, and kidneys, except that theirs are much longer and narrower.

Tail

Kidney

Intestines

Vertebra

Rib

Drops of poison
Scientists "milk" venom from snakes to create a medicine, called antivenin, to neutralize the toxins in a snake's potentially deadly bite.

DIFFERENT BODY TYPES

Although all snakes have a long body, various proportions and shapes match a species' hunting technique and habitat.

Gripping power
Pythons use their thick, muscular body to suffocate prey.

Common shape
The slender garter snake can squeeze into tight places.

Strong swimmer
A paddlelike tail propels sea snakes through water.

Ambush expert
A stout body absorbs the shock from a viper's lightning-fast strike.

Slick and slim
Blind snakes need a smooth, thin body to burrow underground.

Thin climber
A flattened belly helps tree snakes cling to branches.

Flexibility *Pairs of ribs attach to vertebrae with ball-and-socket joints. These connections enable a snake to coil up and flatten its body, and allow side-to-side motion.*

Horn scale

Stomach

Liver

Right lung

Jaw hinge

Upper jaw

Big bite *Gaps between skull bones and the independent movement of both jaws enable a snake to open its mouth incredibly wide. Rows of needle-sharp, angled teeth provide extra grip.*

Fang

Lower jaw

Attack position *Viper fangs lunge forward to strike. Mounted on rotating bones, they fold back into the mouth when not needed. Like all snake teeth, fangs shed regularly and are replaced by new ones.*

Elastic ligament

Tortoises and
Turtles

Tortoises and turtles are the oldest kinds of reptiles and have not changed much in 280 million years. These animals all have a bony shell built into their skeleton. They are divided into two groups based on how they pull their neck into the shell. Hidden-necked turtles bend their neck upward and appear to retract the head straight back, while side-necked turtles fold their neck sideways to bring the head under the shell's rim. About 310 species of tortoises and turtles live in every habitat except the polar regions and high mountains. Most turtles live in or near freshwater, and they have webbed feet and thin shells. More than 50 species of tortoises live on land and have adapted to dry and even desert conditions. Seven kinds of sea turtles come ashore only to lay eggs.

Wraparound neck
Some freshwater species, such as the Australian snake-necked turtle, have a neck that is as long as its body. These turtles live only in the Southern Hemisphere.

Patient attacker
Famous for its swift, savage bite, the alligator snapping turtle of southeastern USA is a fierce predator. It is the heaviest freshwater turtle, with a record shell length of 2.2 feet (67 cm). A snapping turtle lies in wait underwater, then quickly lunges to ambush prey, such as snakes, fish, and birds, killing with its powerful jaws.

MOBILE HOMES

L and turtles often depend entirely on their shells for defense, and their shells tend to be thick and heavy. Many aquatic species have a sleek shell shape that improves swimming speed.

Sealed up
Box turtles can retreat completely inside their hinged shell.

Water dwellers
Most turtles, such as sliders, have a thin, streamlined shell for efficient swimming.

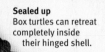

Pig-nosed turtle
The only freshwater turtle with flippers, its shell is covered with tough skin.

Lightweight construction
A sea turtle shell is lightweight but not large enough to hide its head and legs.

Cumbersome covering
A domed shell provides almost total protection, but its weight makes a tortoise slow and clumsy.

Camouflage *An armored shell, covered in algae, and dark skin help hide the turtle on the bottom of a pond. It can stay submerged for more than an hour.*

Cutting edge *Turtles do not have teeth. Instead, sharp jaws made from hornlike material slice food. Some turtles also have a piercing beak. Just like fingernails, turtle jaws grow constantly and never wear out.*

Fishing with worms *These freshwater giants wait for animals to come to them. By wiggling their wormlike tongue lure, they entice unwary fish and other prey within striking distance.*

Claws *Alligator snapping turtles use sturdy claws to grip muddy banks. Females dig nests in dry soil to lay eggs. Webbed feet help these clumsy turtles swim.*

Controlling
Temperature

Reptiles are described as "cold-blooded," but they often have similar body temperatures to mammals and birds. Instead of generating heat internally like other animals, reptiles get their warmth from the Sun and the environment. They move somewhere warm to raise their body temperature and move away from heat to lower it. During winter and cold weather, reptiles allow their body temperature to drop, sometimes close to freezing. They rely on an internal thermostat in their brain, called the pineal gland, to monitor body temperature.

Solar powered

Most reptiles use direct heat from the Sun to raise their body temperature. Small species warm up within a few minutes. Larger reptiles need longer exposure. When a red-headed agama emerges from shelter, it basks on rocks warmed by the Sun. During the day, the lizard's body changes color from drab brown to bright red and blue. To prevent overheating, it moves to cooler surroundings.

HOT-BLOODED TURTLE

Unlike most other reptiles, the leatherback turtle is warmed by its own body heat. When it swims, the movement of its powerful muscles generates heat. A layer of insulating fat keeps the warmth inside the turtle's body. It can survive in water that is too cold for other marine reptiles.

Hot or cold? *A light-sensitive structure on top of the head transmits information to the pineal gland in the brain.*

Early morning *While still cold, lizards cannot run quickly to escape predators. They absorb warmth by pressing their body against sunlight-heated rocks.*

Waking up *The agama is still sluggish as it starts to emerge from an overnight hiding spot. To warm its brain and become fully alert, the lizard first pokes out its head before exposing the rest of its body.*

Gaping jaws
Moisture that evaporates from the open mouth of a black caiman cools blood flowing through its broad tongue.

Fancy footwork
Fringe-toed lizards lift one front leg and the opposite back leg off hot sand, then switch to the other legs to cool their feet.

Late morning *With raised body temperature, the now energetic agama hunts for food. Vivid body colors send a message that the lizard will be hard to catch.*

Afternoon *The lizard seeks shade during the hottest part of the day. Its brilliant colors begin to fade. Still alert, the agama continues to guard its territory and watch for danger.*

Scales and Shells

Tough Cover

Reptiles have dry, tough skin with a thick layer of keratin, the substance that makes fingernails, claws, and feathers. Lizard and snake skin is folded into scales. Crocodilians and some lizards have internal bony plates, called osteoderms, under the tough outer skin layer. Turtles have shells covered by rigid keratin plates that are supported by a bony layer below the shell. From time to time, reptiles shed the outer skin layer. In some reptiles, such as crocodilians and turtles, the old layer constantly flakes off, one plate at a time. In lizards and snakes it comes away in patches or as a complete "peel" of the body—a process called sloughing, or molting.

Shedding skin

To loosen its skin, a corn snake rubs its snout against a rough surface, such as dry grass, rocks, or bark. The old, outer layer detaches and gradually peels off inside-out in one continuous piece. It slides off with the aid of oily fluid that forms between the old layer and new skin beneath.

UNDER THE SURFACE

The epidermis, the outermost layer of skin cells, produces tough keratin. Colored pigment cells, nerves, and blood vessels are located in a deep skin layer called the dermis.

Epidermis

Dermis

Turtle scales
Skin on the head and limbs of turtles is strengthened by tough scalelike folds and plates.

Monitor scales
Small, thick scales are arranged side-by-side in some lizards, such as monitors.

Python scales
Overlapping scales provide extra protection. The soft skin between the scales maintains flexibility.

Osteoderm

Crocodile scales
Bony lumps, called osteoderms, in the dermis give crocodilians armor-plated protection.

Dull start *Before sloughing, the outer skin looks dull as it begins to separate from the layer underneath. The newly exposed skin is brighter than the old, worn skin surface.*

Underside *Snakes have large belly scales with overlapping edges. Similar to treads on a tire, these scales grip the surface a snake moves over.*

Shell anatomy

Turtle shells are made of interconnected bony plates in the dermis and covered by large horny scutes. The upper shell is called the carapace; the lower shell is called the plastron. The backbone and ribs are fused to the carapace.

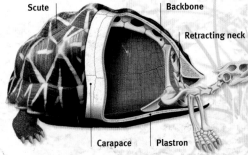

Scute

Backbone

Retracting neck

Carapace

Plastron

Eye protection *The clear, fixed scale, called a brille, that covers a snake's eye is shed with the rest of the skin. The snake's vision will be cloudy for about a week before shedding.*

Colorless *Snakes shed their outer layer of skin in a single piece, starting at the lips. This layer has no color because colored pigment cells are in a deeper layer that is not shed.*

Crack the Egg
A Start in Life

Nearly all reptiles hatch from eggs that can be brittle, like bird shells, or flexible. Most reptile mothers dig a burrow or find a safe hiding place to lay their eggs. A few reptiles make nests by piling up leaves and other plant matter, then guard their eggs while the developing baby, or embryo, matures. The eggs incubate in the warm nest. Sometimes nest temperature determines the sex of the babies. Many species of lizards and snakes give birth to live young that have matured inside the mother. One snake and a small number of lizard species have no males and produce babies that are clones of the mother.

Motherly love

Crocodiles are deadly predators, but they are also the reptile world's most devoted mothers. This female saltwater crocodile, the largest and most dangerous of all, gently carries babies in her mouth from their nest to a sheltered pool. She will take care of them for at least six months.

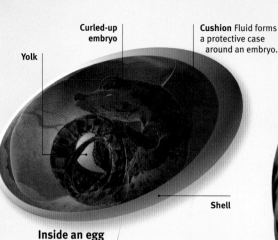

Yolk

Curled-up embryo

Cushion Fluid forms a protective case around an embryo.

Shell

Inside an egg

Crocodile embryos develop for almost 100 days. Each part of an egg helps the embryo survive and grow. One part is a bag of food, the yolk. Other parts store waste or carry oxygen to the embryo.

Baby talk *Still inside the egg, hatching babies call to their mother with high chirps. She responds by scraping away nest material to retrieve her young.*

FINDING A MATE

Female reptiles choose the best males as partners to ensure that their babies will be as healthy as possible. Males use a variety of communication methods, such as displaying their bright colors, to attract females and eliminate other males from the competition.

Press-ups
Male collared lizards perform eye-catching athletic movements and bob up and down to make them look larger and threatening.

Tender touch
A male North American freshwater turtle persistently strokes a female's face with his long claws to demonstrate fitness.

Egg tooth *Hatching reptiles have a spike on the tip of their snout to break through the shell. This "egg tooth" drops off after a few days.*

Soft mouth *By carefully pressing a shell against the roof of her mouth, a mother crocodile can help the babies hatch.*

Defense Tactics
Survival

Most reptiles are small and in danger of being eaten. To avoid this, they have developed a variety of defensive strategies. Many use body color as camouflage to blend into the environment. They move fast and stay close to shelter to disappear quickly from view. If discovered, reptiles commonly bluff and attempt to convince a predator they are dangerous. They puff up with air to look larger, make loud sounds, or threaten to bite. Reptiles that really are dangerous, such as venomous snakes and lizards, advertise this fact with bright colors or distinctive movements. Some harmless species copy these threatening techniques to trick predators into believing they are dangerous as well.

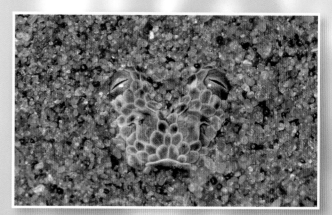

Hidden threat
Some desert snakes shimmy into the sand, leaving only their head exposed. They are almost invisible to predators and can surprise prey.

STRATEGIC MOVES

Reptiles rely on aggression, surprise, trickery, and protective scales to defend themselves. Each species uses its own combination of tactics to prevent becoming a meal for another animal.

Fan out
The frilled lizard extends a skin flap to make its body and head appear wider.

Rolled up
If caught by a predator, the armadillo lizard curls up and turns its spiky scales into a painful mouthful.

Play dead
Some snakes flip over and emit a foul smell to convince a predator that they would not be an appetizing meal.

Sleek shape *A thin body and pointed head enable vine snakes to slip between branches and swiftly hide themselves. Their unique keyhole-shaped pupils give them excellent vision.*

Master of disguise

A vine snake's slender features and green coloring make it nearly invisible against a backdrop of leaves. This camouflage hides the snake from predators and allows it to sneak up on prey. It hunts for food during the day, but even in full sunlight only its movements reveal its presence. If a predator sees the snake, the snake changes appearance to confuse the attacker.

Lethal injection *A vine snake bites down on an animal to force venom through grooves in its rear-pointing fangs. Small teeth keep struggling prey in place.*

Pink inside *Gaping jaws reveal the vine snake's colorful mouth. The goal is to startle a predator. The fangs are too far back and too short to be useful in defense.*

Surprise *When threatened, a vine snake flattens its body from side to side and dramatically exposes black-and-white skin between green scales. The sudden change may distract a predator, giving the snake the opportunity to escape.*

Detecting the World
Senses

Reptiles use similar ways to sense their environment as humans do, including sight, hearing, touch, taste, and smell. Lizards and snakes have an additional sensory structure, called a Jacobson's organ, that allows them to detect chemicals with their tongue. Most reptiles have color vision. Two groups of snakes can "see" prey in the dark using heat sensors. Crocodilians have excellent hearing and detect sounds underwater that other animals cannot hear. Other reptiles hear less well. Snakes, sea turtles, and some lizards do not have external ears, and they pick up vibrations directly with their inner ear.

SIGHT AND TASTE

A range of eyes and tongues suit the way different reptiles gather information.

Large opening
Day-active, or diurnal, reptiles have round pupils and rely on sight to hunt.

Slit opening
Vertical pupils protect a night-active, or nocturnal, reptile's sensitive eyes.

Muscular tongue
A tortoise's thick tongue moves food around in its mouth. Taste buds check the chemicals in food.

Notched tongue
A blunt notch at the end of a slow worm's tongue helps it locate the chemical trail left by prey.

Forked tongue
Both prongs on a tegu's tongue pick up chemicals and give information about a prey's whereabouts.

Combined senses
Snakes rely on numerous sense organs to detect prey. This carpet python has a sensitive nose and a flicking, forked tongue. Vertical pupils in the python's large eyes, well adapted to night vision, open wide in dim light. Heat receptors on its lower lips and nose enable the python to locate warm-blooded prey, such as mammals, in total darkness.

Exposed eardrum
Most lizards have simpler and less sensitive ears than mammals. In some lizards, such as a bearded dragon, the eardrum is a skin-covered depression visible on its head.

Jacobson's organ

When a snake retracts its tongue, it wipes the forked tips over tubes that lead to the Jacobson's organ. This organ, a dense cluster of cells on the roof of the mouth, analyzes particles on the tongue and sends information to the snake's brain.

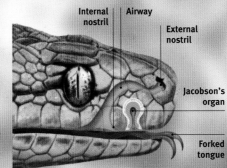

Internal nostril

Airway

External nostril

Jacobson's organ

Forked tongue

Feel the heat *Pythons, pit vipers, and boas have heat-sensitive pits that detect tiny temperature differences. They tell a snake what direction prey is in and even the location of the heart, an animal's warmest part.*

Seeing *Snakes do not have movable eyelids so they cannot blink. Their eyes are covered by a special clear scale. Python pupils close to a thin slit in bright light to protect their eyes.*

Smelling *External nostrils pick up airborne scents that can travel a long way from their source. These smells provide an early warning about what is approaching the snake's surroundings.*

Tasting *Snakes flick their tongue in and out to collect particles from the air, water, or ground. These chemicals can help snakes locate food, avoid predators, or follow the trail of possible mates.*

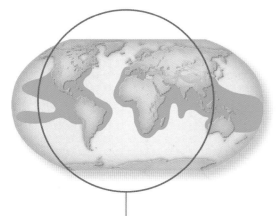

HAWKSBILL TURTLE: THE FACTS

SCIENTIFIC NAME: *Eretmochelys imbricata*

ORDER: Testudinata

FAMILY: Chelonidae

HABITAT: Shallow tropical seas

DIET: Sponges, sea squirts

CONSERVATION STATUS: Endangered

Fast facts Fast facts at your fingertips give you essential information on each featured reptile.

Locator map The green shading on this map of the world shows you where the featured reptile lives.

Species bar This bar shows which category the reptile belongs to.

CROCODILIANS

LIZARDS

SNAKES

TORTOISES AND TURTLES

NILE CROCODILE: THE FACTS

SCIENTIFIC NAME: *Crocodylus niloticus*

ORDER: Crocodilia

FAMILY: Crocodylidae

HABITAT: Freshwater rivers, lakes, swamps

DIET: Insects, frogs, fish, birds, reptiles, mammals

CONSERVATION STATUS: Threatened

10-year-old boy
4.5 ft (1.4 m)

Nile crocodile
16.5 ft (5 m)

Nile Crocodile

Death Roll

One of the world's fiercest carnivores, the Nile crocodile has no enemies apart from other crocodiles, hippopotamuses, and humans. Almost invisible when lying motionless under murky water, they attack with a powerful lunge to capture land-dwelling animals that come to the river's edge to drink. Crocodile jaws are a monstrous trap designed to shatter bones. Their teeth do not cut, so they must tear off large pieces of meat. Small prey is swallowed whole. Once a crocodile has gorged itself, it may not need to eat again for many months and survives on fat stored in its muscular tail.

Feeding frenzy
Crocodiles swarm around a lone zebra. If a victim escapes from one set of powerful jaws, another can make the kill. Large prey provide enough food for several crocodiles to feast on.

Underbelly *Crocodiles do not chew their food. Like birds, they have a double stomach to aid digestion. Stones, called gastroliths, in the first stomach grind down chunks of flesh, which are then digested in the highly acidic second stomach.*

Prey *Using stealth and speed, determined crocodiles ambush migrating animals during river crossings. Wildebeest weigh about 600 pounds (275 kg), approximately half the weight of a male Nile crocodile.*

Piercing jaws *Large, adult crocodiles exert a pressure of 1–2 tons (1–2 t) with their mouth, enough to crush an animal's skull. Their teeth frequently break but are replaced by new ones that push up through the old.*

Twist and turn

With tremendous force, a Nile crocodile pivots its entire body and thrashes a doomed wildebeest against the water to rip it into bite-sized chunks. This "death roll" ensures that large prey is too confused to struggle free and quickly causes lethal injuries. On dry land many mammals could outrun a crocodile, so a preferred killing method is to drag animals into the water to drown them.

MOUTH FULL OF WATER

When partially submerged, two throat flaps block the crocodile's windpipe to prevent drowning. Internal nostrils transport air behind the flaps so it can still breathe.

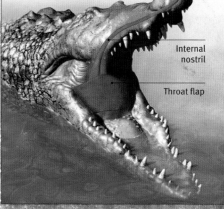

Internal nostril

Throat flap

TORTOISES AND TURTLES   SNAKES   LIZARDS   CROCODILIANS

Fast fishing

Gharials flick their head sideways with great speed to catch fish. Most of their head is close to the flexible neck joint.

GHARIAL: THE FACTS

SCIENTIFIC NAME: *Gavialis gangeticus*

ORDER: Crocodilia

FAMILY: Gavialidae

HABITAT: Slow-flowing rivers, streams

DIET: Fish, insects, frogs, small aquatic animals

CONSERVATION STATUS: Endangered

Gharial

On the Nose

Two crocodilians are highly specialized fish killers. The best known is the gharial, which lives in large rivers in India and adjacent countries. The gharial gets its name from the knob on the tip of a male's snout, called a "ghara," meaning pot in Hindi. A smaller relative, called the false gharial, lives in Borneo. Gharials don't hunt dangerous prey, and they are less aggressive and have weaker legs than other crocodilians. To catch a meal, gharials attack with swift, sideways strikes as fish swim by. Their long, narrow snout slices through water and their sharp teeth are perfect for snagging slippery fish.

CROCODILES IN MOTION

On land, almost all crocodilians are slow and awkward. Their tail is a burden and they rely on short legs to hunt and escape danger. A few small crocodilian species can gallop at 10 miles per hour (16 km/h), but only for short distances.

Raised up

Most crocodilians use a "high walk," with the body arched up and limbs extended. The heavy tail drags on the ground.

River's edge

Gharials usually crawl on their belly to get from the riverbank into the water, then slide in, hardly making a splash. They lose body heat hunting fish in cool water. Periodically, they come ashore to warm up, or bask. Reptiles digest food more efficiently when their body temperature is high.

Sandy banks

In winter, gharials spend a lot of time out of the water. A female gharial digs a nest in the sand and lays up to 50 eggs. She will guard her eggs until they hatch 60–80 days later.

Powered swimming

Like all crocodilians, gharials move gracefully through water, propelled by the side-to-side movement of their tail.

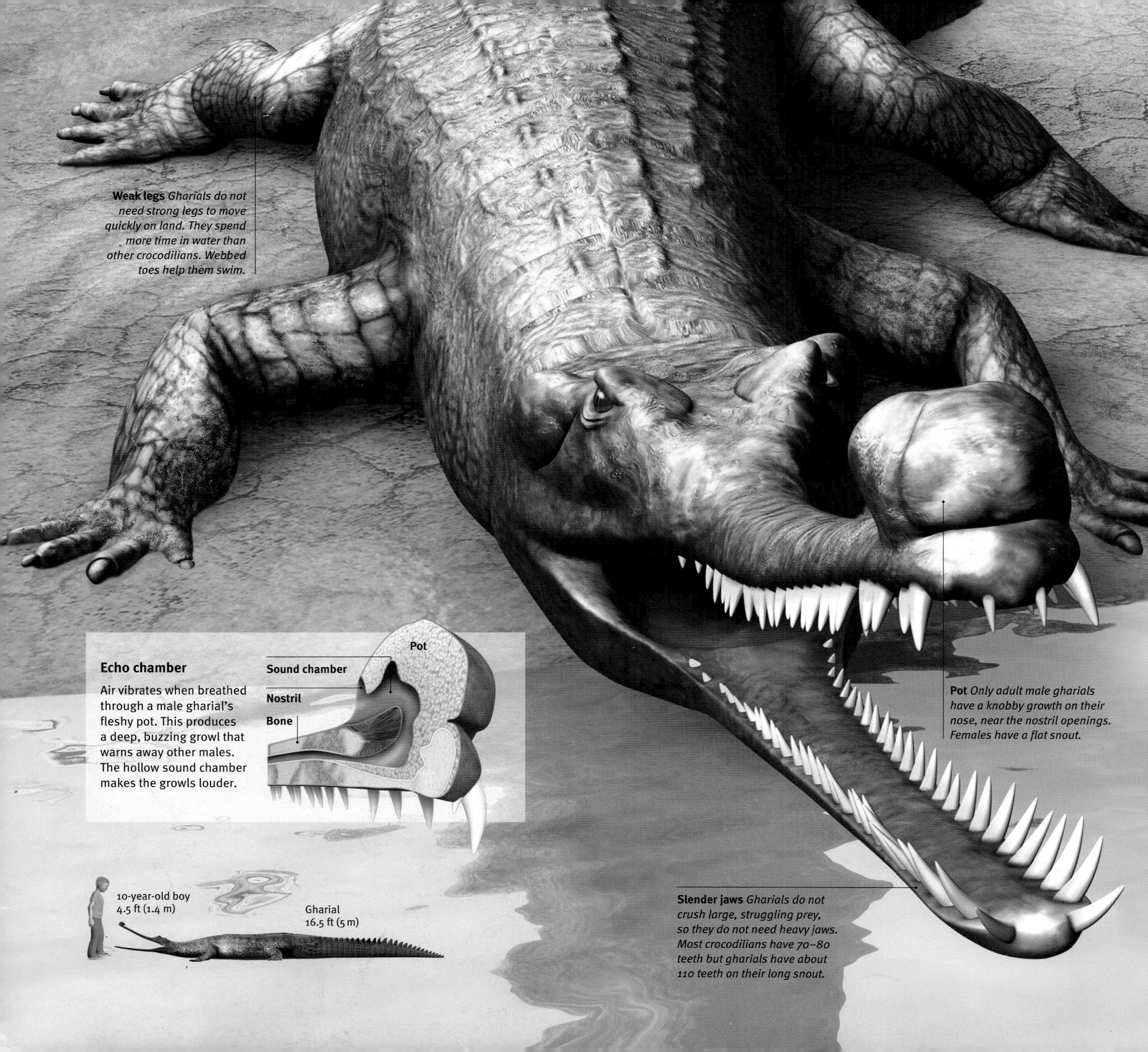

Pot *Only adult male gharials have a knobby growth on their nose, near the nostril openings. Females have a flat snout.*

Slender jaws *Gharials do not crush large, struggling prey, so they do not need heavy jaws. Most crocodilians have 70–80 teeth but gharials have about 110 teeth on their long snout.*

Weak legs *Gharials do not need strong legs to move quickly on land. They spend more time in water than other crocodilians. Webbed toes help them swim.*

Echo chamber

Air vibrates when breathed through a male gharial's fleshy pot. This produces a deep, buzzing growl that warns away other males. The hollow sound chamber makes the growls louder.

Pot

Sound chamber

Nostril

Bone

Gharial
16.5 ft (5 m)

10-year-old boy
4.5 ft (1.4 m)

CROCODILIANS

LIZARDS

SNAKES

TORTOISES AND TURTLES

GILA MONSTER: THE FACTS

SCIENTIFIC NAME: *Heloderma suspectum*

ORDER: Squamata

FAMILY: Helodermatidae

HABITAT: Deserts

DIET: Eggs, nestlings, small mammals

CONSERVATION STATUS: Stable

10-year-old boy
4.5 ft (1.4 m)

Gila monster
2 ft (60 cm)

Gila Monster

Toxic Bite

Gila monsters are specialized desert dwellers that forage for nutritious eggs and feed on litters of young animals, such as rats and ground squirrels. These slow lizards are vulnerable to attack, but their venomous bite is a powerful deterrent to predators. They have long, sharp teeth and a blunt head with tremendously powerful jaw muscles. Their venom is not fatal to humans but it causes incredible pain, tissue damage, and dizziness. Scientists have discovered that a component in Gila monster venom can be made into a medicine to help diabetics.

ALL IN THE FAMILY

Several lizard families related to Gila monsters and snakes have venom glands. Best known are monitor lizards. Their venom can destroy body tissue.

Sand monitor
Monitors are energetic lizards with a venomous bite, strong sense of smell, and keen sight.

Komodo dragon
The world's largest lizard kills mammals, such as deer and goats, with bacteria-filled saliva.

Mexican beaded lizard
Close relatives of Gila monsters, these lizards spend most of the day in burrows to avoid the heat.

On the prowl

Gila monsters search for food in the late afternoon and early evening to avoid the hottest part of the day. When threatened, these lizards open their mouth and expose sharp teeth to scare off attackers. They will bite only as a last resort.

Energy supply *The thick tail contains a large reserve of fat. Gila monsters are able to survive for several months without food.*

Lethal glands *The venom glands in Gila monsters are located in the lower jaw. Several outlets from the gland drain into the tissue at the base of the teeth.*

Bumpy skin *Beadlike scales form a Gila monster's tough covering. Its muscular limbs, stocky body, and sharp claws enable it to break into other animals' nests and burrows.*

Venom flood *Gila monsters do not inject venom. Instead, their venom oozes out along grooved gutters on several lower teeth. The longer the lizard chews, the more of its slow-acting venom is forced into the prey's wounds.*

CROCODILIANS

LIZARDS

SNAKES

TORTOISES AND TURTLES

TOKAY GECKO: THE FACTS

SCIENTIFIC NAME: *Gecko gecko*

ORDER: Squamata

FAMILY: Gekkonidae

HABITAT: Tropical forests, woodlands, buildings

DIET: Insects, spiders, lizards, frogs

CONSERVATION STATUS: Stable

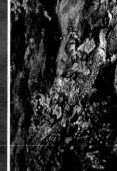

Tokay gecko
1.1 ft (35 cm)

Boy's hand
6 in (15 cm)

Spot the lizard
Australian leaf-tailed geckos use their concealing color and texture to hide in plain sight.

Tokay Gecko

Sticky Feet

Tokay geckos are one of the largest gecko species. They are also one of the noisiest. They get their name from the barking call they make, a loud "tok–kaaay, tok–kaaay," to let other animals know they are nearby. They defend their territory, and if their warning sounds do not scare away intruders, vicious fights may break out. Like many geckos, these lizards are able to cling to walls and walk upside down. Their toe pads grip onto a surface's invisible rough patches. Tokay geckos have exceptionally good vision, and they do not blink. Their eyes are protected by a transparent scale instead of eyelids.

STUCK TOGETHER

E ach female gecko lays two eggs at a time. When first laid, the eggs are sticky. Occasionally, females will share a good nesting site. They glue their eggs to well-protected, vertical surfaces, such as tree hollows, away from predators.

Lose the tail *Mammals and snakes prey on tokay geckos. Like many kinds of lizards, if caught, tokay geckos can break off their tail to escape.*

Hanging on *Needle-sharp claws help geckos cling to tree branches, especially in wet weather when sticky toe pads do not work well.*

Toes *The underside of each toe has a layer of overlapping pads, which are covered with millions of microscopic hairs.*

Under the microscope *Tiny hairs on a gecko's toe end in a cluster of flattened disks, which act like suction cups.*

Fine tuning *Geckos have the best hearing of all lizards. Inside the ear opening is a delicate eardrum, connected to a sensitive middle ear.*

Eyesight *A tokay gecko's pupil has ragged edges, instead of being a straight slit. In bright light, their pupils close to a series of pinholes that reduce glare and sharpen focus.*

Licked clean *Clear vision is vital to a tokay gecko. It regularly wipes its tongue over the fixed scale, or spectacle, that covers each eye.*

Night life

Tokay geckos are nocturnal and become active shortly after sunset. Sometimes, they lurk near buildings to hunt animals that are attracted to a glowing light. Geckos stalk prey using catlike movements, then catch it with a rapid, final dash. Most gecko species eat only insects and spiders, but an adult tokay gecko will feed on frogs and small lizards as well.

CROCODILIANS

LIZARDS

SNAKES

TORTOISES AND TURTLES

REGAL HORNED LIZARD: THE FACTS

SCIENTIFIC NAME:	*Phrynosoma solare*
ORDER:	Squamata
FAMILY:	Phrynosomatidae
HABITAT:	Stony deserts
DIET:	Ants, insects, spiders
CONSERVATION STATUS:	Stable

Regal horned lizard
5 in (13 cm)

Boy's hand
6 in (15 cm)

Regal Horned Lizard

Blood Squirt

Horned lizards are a diverse group that thrive in rocky deserts. They hibernate in underground burrows during freezing winter months. Regal horned lizards are small and have several ways of avoiding predators. In daylight, their coloring and shape provide camouflage. Overnight they bury themselves in sand. During the day, they hunt for ants, their main food source. Because ants are not very nutritious and are hard to digest, regal horned lizards must eat huge numbers of them. The lizard sits patiently beside ant trails and licks up the insects with its sticky tongue.

Regal horned lizard

Thorny devil

Seeing is believing

Seen from the outside, both regal horned lizards and thorny devils have spikes on their head. But their skulls show that a regal horned lizard's spikes are bone, whereas a thorny devil's are only enlarged body scales attached to its skin.

Irritating stream

The regal horned lizard has a bizarre defense method. When threatened by a coyote or fox, the lizard forces a stream of blood from its eye. The spray reaches as far as 4 feet (1.2 m) away. The blood stream contains fluids that can irritate the predator's eyes, nose, or mouth. The liquid may also have a bad smell or taste.

IN EMERGENCY, DROP TAIL!

Most lizards can shed all or part of their tail to escape danger. If a tail is grabbed or hit, a vertebra fractures along an area of weakness and tail muscles pull in opposite directions. A replacement tail, which is usually plain colored, regrows from the stump.

Clean break
The tail comes off with minimal loss of blood.

Sharp mouthful *Head horns and spiny scales on their squat, rounded body make these lizards difficult to swallow. Their texture and mottled colors blend in with the rocky ground.*

Bursting out *Regal horned lizards have a blood-filled chamber beneath each eye where several veins join. When valves that restrict blood flow in the head clamp shut, mounting blood pressure bursts the chamber.*

CROCODILIANS

LIZARDS

SNAKES

TORTOISES AND TURTLES

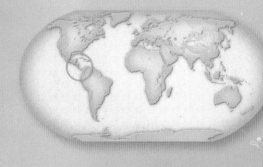

GREEN BASILISK: THE FACTS

SCIENTIFIC NAME: *Basilisk plumifrons*

ORDER: Squamata

FAMILY: Corytophanidae

HABITAT: Tropical forest

DIET: Plants, insects, small vertebrates

CONSERVATION STATUS: Endangered

10-year-old boy
4.5 ft (1.4 m)

Green basilisk
3 ft (90 cm)

Green Basilisk

Run on Water

The largest and most colorful of the four basilisk species is the green basilisk from Nicaragua and Honduras. Basilisks, a kind of iguana, are versatile forest dwellers that can run, climb, and swim with equal ease. The ability of these lizards to run on the surface of water is the reason for their local name, Jesus lizards. When running at high speed, they stand nearly upright on their rear legs. If they need to hide, they can stay underwater for 30 minutes or longer. Only male green basilisks have elaborate crests along the back and tail that they use to advertise their presence. Females are similar in size but much less conspicuous. Sailback lizards of Indonesia and the Philippines also run on water using fringed toe scales.

Tail *A long tail shifts the center of balance to the basilisk's hips during its sprint on water. This helps the lizard run upright.*

ADAPTED FOR SAND

Web-footed geckos need to move on shifting sand dunes in desert regions. The fine webbing that joins the toes makes their feet broader so they do not sink into the sand.

Desert gecko Webbed feet provide snowshoelike support for moving on sand.

Quick dash

When alarmed, a basilisk can run swiftly across the surface of a stream or pond to escape. This unusual ability is based on speed and the specialized fringed scales on its toes that make them wider and flatter than other lizards' toes. Each toe pushes back against the water and propels the lizard forward.

Gripping tips *Basilisks are agile climbers. Sharp claws dig into bark and help them scurry up trees.*

Sink and swim

Basilisks are strong swimmers and use their crested tail for propulsion. In the water, they move like small crocodiles, holding their limbs flat against the body.

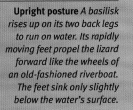

Upright posture *A basilisk rises up on its two back legs to run on water. Its rapidly moving feet propel the lizard forward like the wheels of an old-fashioned riverboat. The feet sink only slightly below the water's surface.*

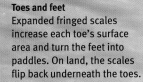

Toes and feet
Expanded fringed scales increase each toe's surface area and turn the feet into paddles. On land, the scales flip back underneath the toes.

Wrapped around *The prehensile tail can coil around twigs to anchor the chameleon. The tail cannot be shed if pulled.*

Locked in combat
Jackson's chameleons are one of several species that have horns. Males lock horns as a test of strength during the mating season. The first to fall off loses.

CAPE DWARF CHAMELEON: THE FACTS

SCIENTIFIC NAME: *Bradypodion pumilum*

ORDER: **Squamata**

FAMILY: **Chamaeleonidae**

HABITAT: **Open woodland, gardens**

DIET: **Insects, spiders**

CONSERVATION STATUS: **Stable**

Cape Dwarf Chameleon
Quick Change

Chameleons change color faster and with more variety than any other lizards. Their most dramatic color changes are used to communicate with other chameleons. Specific colors and patterns distinguish males from females, and indicate readiness to mate or willingness to fight. Sudden flashes of color can startle an enemy. Chameleon skin cells make a broader range of colors than the human eye can detect. Other chameleon specialties include independently moving eyes, toes that grasp, and an incredibly long tongue.

COLOR SIGNALS

The transparent skin of a chameleon has layers of pigment cells: yellow, red, blue, and brown. They work together to produce various color combinations.

Pigment cells
Dark brown melanin cells either contract to reveal or branch out to cover the other cells. This changes the chameleon's colors.

Different looks
Two patches of panther chameleon skin show the camouflaged state on the left and warning colors on the right.

Rotating turrets *Each eye can swivel separately from the other. Lenses magnify and focus to measure the distance to prey.*

Sticky tongue *Chameleon tongues are covered with sticky saliva. The tip puckers to trap prey. Mouth muscles shoot the tongue forward, often faster than 16 feet (5 m) per second.*

Grasping hands *On all four feet, chameleons have two sets of partially fused toes that grip with a pincer action.*

Hold tight

Like all chameleons, even the few that live on the ground, the Cape dwarf chameleon is built to roam in trees. Its flattened body is not much wider than a twig, the feet are perfect graspers, and its tail acts like a fifth limb when climbing.

Cape dwarf chameleon
6 in (15 cm)

Boy's hand
6 in (15 cm)

MARINE IGUANA: THE FACTS

SCIENTIFIC NAME: *Amblyrhynchus cristatus*

ORDER: Squamata

FAMILY: Iguanidae

HABITAT: Galápagos Islands

DIET: Marine algae

CONSERVATION STATUS: Stable

10-year-old boy
4.5 ft (1.4 m)

Marine iguana
4 ft (1.2 m)

Tail power *Marine iguanas use their flattened tail for propulsion and steering when swimming, just like crocodiles. For efficiency and speed, the limbs are held close against the body.*

Marine Iguana

Island Life

Many lizards are good swimmers and some live on the coast, but the marine iguana is the only species that needs to swim under the sea to find food. They live only on the Galápagos, arid and rocky islands with little vegetation. The cold waters around the islands are rich in sea life, and these herbivores have adapted to eat underwater plants. They dive into the ocean and feed until their air runs out or they get too cold. To raise their body temperature, groups of marine iguanas congregate on the shore, basking on dark rocks—and even on top of each other—to absorb warmth from the Sun.

GALÁPAGOS CONSERVATION

Many kinds of plants and animals are unique to the Galápagos Islands. Efforts are under way to protect vulnerable species and the environment.

Sole survivor
Only one male Pinta Island tortoise is still alive, Lonesome George. There is hope that genetically similar animals might live on a nearby island and could produce offspring with him.

Tight grip *Powerful claws cling to underwater rocks against the pull of waves and currents.*

Below the surface

A marine iguana feeds by pressing its blunt snout close to rocks to bite off algae. Staying submerged in chilly water lowers its body temperature. As it cools, the lizard reduces blood flow to the legs and tail so warmth is directed to its brain and vital organs. Adults are able to hold their breath for 40–60 minutes and can dive to a maximum of 50 feet (15 m).

Salty spray

Marine iguanas take in large amounts of salt from their food. They shed the excess using a special gland in the nose and sneeze away concentrated brine.

Diving down *Marine iguanas usually feed in 5–15 feet (1.5–4.5 m) of water. Only adults stay warm long enough and have the strength to dive deeply. Juveniles eat algae exposed at low tide or do shallow dives.*

Color signals *Marine iguanas are usually a grayish black. In breeding season, the male's limbs turn green and its sides become rusty red. This tells females he is ready to mate.*

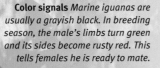

Razor-sharp teeth

Each marine iguana tooth has three pointy blades. The teeth line up along the jaw to create a serrated edge that slices food.

CROCODILIANS

LIZARDS

SNAKES

TORTOISES AND TURTLES

Vestigial limbs
Pythons and boas are the only snakes with remnants of hind limbs that look like small claws.

Burmese Python
Squeeze Tight

The largest living snakes are the pythons and boas, two related groups that specialize as constrictors. Both snakes wrap body coils around prey and use powerful muscles to squeeze it to death. Adult Burmese pythons weigh about 100 pounds (45 kg) and can grow up to 20 feet (6 m) long. Only the reticulated python, the anaconda (a boa), and the African rock python are bigger. Female pythons guard their eggs and will not eat until they hatch. If the eggs get too cool, the mother python shivers to generate body warmth to raise the temperature of the eggs.

BURMESE PYTHON: THE FACTS

SCIENTIFIC NAME: *Python molurus bivittatus*

ORDER: Squamata

FAMILY: Boidae

HABITAT: Tropical forests, woodlands, swamps

DIET: Mammals, birds, reptiles

CONSERVATION STATUS: Stable

Burmese python
20 ft (6 m)

10-year-old boy
4.5 ft (1.4 m)

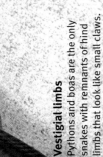

EGG SPECIALIST

African egg-eating snakes have few teeth. They swallow a bird's egg whole and cut it open with spiky vertebrae in their throat. They regurgitate the shell after draining the contents.

Big meal

An adult Burmese python can eat a young Siamese crocodile whole. Once the crocodile is unconscious or dead, the python relaxes its grip and swallows the prey headfirst. The python then "walks" its jaws forward bit by bit until the entire body is inside. Digesting a large animal can take weeks or months.

Looped coils *Large prey is killed by suffocation. Every time the crocodile exhales, the snake wraps the coils tighter to stop its prey from inhaling.*

Breathing *When the mouth is blocked, the snake projects its windpipe out beyond the prey to continue breathing while it swallows.*

Jaws *The jaws are each split in half and both sides work independently of the other.*

Hinge *The quadrate bone has the hinge for the lower jaw. A python is able to open its mouth wider than other reptiles can because this long bone is located far back on the skull.*

CROCODILIANS

LIZARDS

SNAKES

TORTOISES AND TURTLES

WESTERN DIAMONDBACK RATTLESNAKE: THE FACTS

SCIENTIFIC NAME: *Crotalus atrox*

ORDER: Squamata

FAMILY: Viperidae

HABITAT: Dry woodland and desert scrub

DIET: Small mammals, especially rodents

CONSERVATION STATUS: Stable

10-year-old boy
4.5 ft (1.4 m)

Western diamondback
rattlesnake 5 ft (1.5 m)

Western Diamondback Rattlesnake

Warning Sound

One of the biggest and most dangerous of the 33 species of rattlesnakes is the western diamondback. Rattlesnakes, like other pit vipers, have long, venom-injecting fangs and heat-sensitive pits on the snout that detect warm-blooded animals in the dark. A western diamondback rattlesnake's venom breaks down soft body tissue and blood vessels, causing shock and unconsciousness. It strikes with great speed at prey, usually mice or rats, and uses its forked tongue to follow the scent trail to where the prey has died.

Open wide

A rattlesnake's bite is dangerous to many animals. Rattlesnakes mainly use venom for killing food. With their color pattern as camouflage, they hide from sight among dried leaves. When in danger of being trampled or attacked, rattlesnakes send out a loud warning buzz using their rattle to scare off intruders.

Shaking it *Every time a rattlesnake sheds its skin, a hollow, button-shaped scale is left behind on the tail. After several sheds, the tip of the tail becomes a set of hard, dry "shells."*

SNAKE KILLERS

Certain animals have developed immunity or resistance to snake venom and can survive bites that would kill other species. Collared lizards, kingsnakes, and some ground squirrels are resistant to a rattlesnake's potent venom.

Speed and agility
Mongoose are resistant to cobra venom. They are rarely bitten as they outmaneuver the snake, killing it with a bite to the head.

Deadly step
Secretary birds kill snakes by whacking them against the ground or stomping on them.

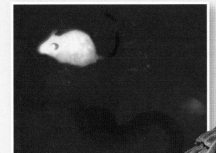

Warm target
Even in total darkness, heat-sensing pits enable a rattlesnake to detect prey's body warmth.

Swing action *Rattlesnake fangs rotate forward to strike. The thin, fleshy sheath slides back as the rattlesnake bites. When the mouth is closed, the long fangs lie flat against the roof of its mouth.*

Quick lunge *Ambush predators move with lightning-fast speed when they strike. A rattlesnake's muscular body provides a solid launching pad for the head and neck to shoot forward.*

CROCODILIANS

LIZARDS

SNAKES

TORTOISES AND TURTLES

BANDED SEA KRAIT: THE FACTS

SCIENTIFIC NAME: *Laticauda colubrina*

ORDER: Squamata

FAMILY: Elapidae

HABITAT: Tropical and subtropical oceans

DIET: Fish

CONSERVATION STATUS: Not endangered

10-year-old boy
4.5 ft (1.4 m)

Banded sea krait
3 ft (90 cm)

Banded Sea Krait
Life in Water

Two groups of snakes thrive in saltwater environments: semi-aquatic sea kraits that split their time between land and water, and true sea snakes that spend all their time in the sea. Both groups evolved from the elapid family of snakes, which includes cobras. Underwater adaptations for sea species include nostrils that shut to keep out water and flattened tails for efficient swimming. Banded sea kraits come ashore often on coral islands to bask in the sun for warmth. Unlike true sea snakes that give birth at sea to litters of live young, sea kraits venture onto land to find a sheltered spot above the waterline to lay their eggs.

HOW SNAKES MOVE

Snakes have developed several different ways of getting around without limbs. Most move by wiggling their flexible backbone from side to side with lateral undulations. Muscles send S-shaped waves along the body from front to back. Rough belly scales help push the snake forward.

S-shaped movement
When a snake can press against something, it moves rapidly forward.

Concertina movement
The snake extends its head forward to find an anchor point, then draws the rest of the body up.

Caterpillar movement
Some heavy-bodied snakes generate ripples down the belly to move straight ahead.

Sidewinding movement
Desert vipers anchor their head and tail, then throw coils of their body sideways to move across loose sand.

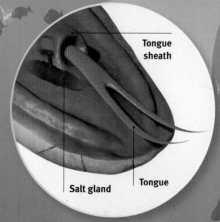

Tongue
sheath

Salt gland

Tongue

Excess salt *A salt gland under a sea krait's tongue concentrates the salt that enters its body, then releases it back into the water as brine. The gland opens into the tongue sheath, so every flick of the snake's tongue pushes out some salt.*

Surface breathers *As their nostrils are located on top of the snout, sea kraits do not have to lift their entire head out of water to take in air. A large lung capacity enables them to stay underwater for more than an hour, but they usually surface to breathe every 10–20 minutes.*

Slippery mouthful *A sea krait injects venom with short fangs and hangs on so the fish does not float away. The snake's jaws stretch to swallow something wider than its head. Prey is digested whole, bones and all.*

Feeding frenzy

Banded sea kraits sometimes converge near coral reefs to hunt fish and look for a mate. Sea kraits inherited highly toxic, nerve-poisoning venom from their land-dwelling ancestors. Just a tiny drop of the powerful venom is enough to paralyze and kill a fish almost instantly.

Push power *All sea kraits have a flat tail that makes them fast swimmers. They push the sides of their body against the water. Their round body shape and enlarged belly scales are needed for crawling on land.*

CROCODILIANS

LIZARDS

SNAKES

TORTOISES AND TURTLES

Red Spitting Cobra
In Your Eye

The red spitting cobra lives in the deserts of Africa. Like all 32 cobra species, it has a characteristic threat display. It raises its upper body off the ground and extends its neck ribs to intimidate attackers. The short, fixed fangs of all cobras deliver powerful venom, which acts on the nerves of its attackers to stop their heart and damage their lungs. Several kinds of cobras can "spit" venom at the eyes of predators, such as large mammals and birds of prey. Red spitting cobras hunt both day and night for rodents and toads. They will sometimes bite in self-defense.

Blinding spray

All species of spitting cobras have developed an advanced defense system. They can aim a stream of venom at the eyes of their attacker. A forceful exhale turns the jet into a fine mist. Even a small drop of the venom causes instant pain and inflammation when it hits the surface of the eye. The venom is so toxic that only a tiny amount is needed to kill or disable prey.

RED SPITTING COBRA: THE FACTS

SCIENTIFIC NAME: *Naja pallida*

ORDER: **Squamata**

FAMILY: **Elapidae**

HABITAT: **Dry subtropical woodlands and savannas**

DIET: **Small mammals, frogs, toads**

CONSERVATION STATUS: **Stable**

Venom gland

Fang *The oval opening at the tip of a cobra's hollow fang faces forward. The cobra contracts muscles surrounding the venom gland to force a jet of venom through the hole.*

Extended hood *Cobras have unusually long, pivoting neck ribs. Muscles stretch the ribs sideways and fan out the skin into a "hood," giving cobra necks their spoonlike shape.*

Threat pose *Cobras rear up when alarmed or disturbed, not to attack prey. The display makes them easier to see and warns approaching animals.*

Harmless mimic
The Asian false cobra lacks front fangs and powerful venom, but poses like a real cobra to deter attackers.

Charming cobras
Snakes have trouble hearing airborne sounds, such as music. Snake charmers mesmerize cobras with the swaying motion of the flute.

10-year-old boy
4-5 ft (1.4 m)

Red spitting cobra
4 ft (1.2 m)

CROCODILIANS

LIZARDS

SNAKES

TORTOISES AND TURTLES

RED-FOOTED TORTOISE: THE FACTS

SCIENTIFIC NAME: *Geochelone carbonaria*

ORDER: Testudinata

FAMILY: Testudinae

HABITAT: Rain forests, tropical woodlands, savannas

DIET: Leaves, flowers, fruits

CONSERVATION STATUS: Stable

10-year-old boy
4.5 ft (1.4 m)

Red-footed tortoise
1.1 ft (35 cm)

Tough cover *Predators have difficulty biting a tortoise's hard, rounded shell. When threatened, the tortoise can retract its head and limbs out of reach into the shell.*

Red-footed Tortoise

Tip Over

Red-footed tortoises live in tropical environments, unlike most land tortoises that live in dry or even desert regions. Adults weight about 15 pounds (7 kg). A massive, domed shell protects tortoises from attack. The shell is heavy and awkward, and it prevents them from moving quickly. Red-footed tortoises are herbivores and eat only plants. They use their horned jaws to break off leaves and flowers from shrubs. They are closely related to, but much smaller than, the giant tortoises of the Galápagos Islands.

TURTLE DEFENSES

To discourage animals from attacking, American stink-pots release foul-smelling, skunklike chemicals. Most aquatic turtle species are able to swim quickly to avoid predators.

Rough edges
Some species of turtles are born with a sharp, spiky ridge on the shell to protect them from predatory fish.

Shut tight
The underside, or plastron, of a box turtle's shell has a hinge. The turtle can firmly close its shell, like lifting up a drawbridge, with the head and limbs safely inside.

Fighting tactics

Male tortoises compete with other males over territory and to win access to females. In battle they ram their opponent, and one tortoise may be knocked onto its side. Although a tortoise can usually turn back over, it is an exhausting process. If the day is hot and the tortoise takes too long to right itself, it might overheat in the scorching sun and die.

Fierce bite *When fighting, a tortoise will bite the rival's vulnerable head, neck, and limbs with its pointed beak and sharp-edged jaws.*

Sturdy support *Tortoise legs need to be stocky to carry the weight of its heavy shell. Females use their short, strong claws to dig nesting holes for their 5–15 eggs.*

Matched curves *A male tortoise has an inwardly curved plastron that fits against a female's domed shell, or carapace, during reproduction. The female has a flat plastron.*

CROCODILIANS

LIZARDS

SNAKES

TORTOISES AND TURTLES

HAWKSBILL TURTLE: THE FACTS

SCIENTIFIC NAME: *Eretmochelys imbricata*

ORDER: Testudinata

FAMILY: Chelonidae

HABITAT: Shallow tropical seas

DIET: Sponges, sea squirts

CONSERVATION STATUS: Endangered

10-year-old boy
4.5 ft (1.4 m)

Hawksbill turtle
3.3 ft (1 m)

Hawksbill Turtle
Coral Living

The hawksbill turtle is one of seven species of sea turtles. Streamlined sea turtle shells are thinner and lighter than those of land turtles. Their limbs are modified as flippers, adapted for marine life. Front flippers provide power, while broad rear flippers lift and steer. Unlike other sea turtles, hawksbills do not make long migrations from feeding areas to nesting sites. Hawksbill turtles hatch from eggs laid on tropical beaches. Males never return to shore. Females return to the beach where they hatched to lay 90–190 eggs. Nest temperature determines the sex of the babies. Adults have few enemies, besides sharks and humans.

ENDANGERED SPECIES

Sea turtle numbers are declining. They have been hunted for their meat, shells, and eggs. Trapped in nets or ropes, they drown. Fragile nesting beaches are destroyed by development.

Bleached coral
Coral reefs are in danger from rising sea temperature.

Tortoiseshell products
Hawksbills were once killed for their lovely translucent scales.

Deadly rubbish
Leatherbacks mistake plastic bags for jellyfish and choke to death.

Race to the water
Hatching is the most dangerous time for sea turtles. They rely on safety in numbers during their journey to the ocean. Predators on land and below the surface feed on baby turtles. Few survive to become adults.

Cleaning crew *Cleaner wrasse scour off barnacles and other sea life that grow on sea turtles and large marine animals. These fish stop the shells from becoming overgrown with parasites.*

Service station

Hawksbills stay close to coral reefs for feeding. They slice up marine sponges, their main food source, with their sharp beak. They are attracted to groups of brightly colored cleaner fish. The turtles even line up sometimes, waiting patiently for their turn to be cleaned by schools of fish.

Bony paddle *Short, thick arm bones and long fingers inside the flipper support powerful swimming movements.*

Reptile Family Tree

Classifying reptiles

Species are categorized into groups according to how closely related they are to one another. Members of each group can be identified as such because they share a number of body features. In this way, scientists organize information about the diversity of life.

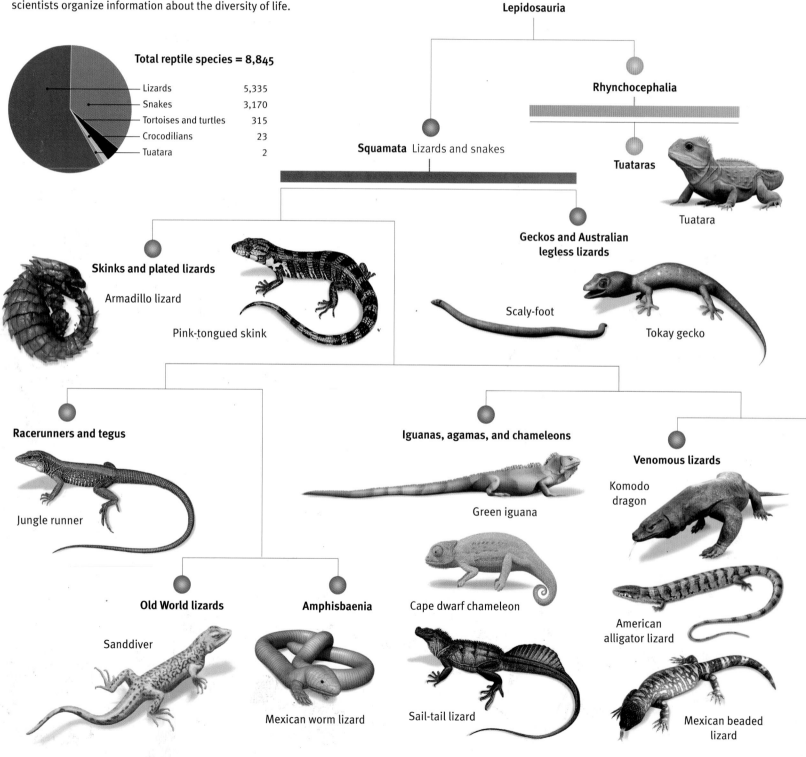

Total reptile species = 8,845

Lizards	5,335
Snakes	3,170
Tortoises and turtles	315
Crocodilians	23
Tuatara	2

Lepidosauria

Rhynchocephalia

Squamata Lizards and snakes

Tuataras

Tuatara

Skinks and plated lizards

Armadillo lizard

Pink-tongued skink

Geckos and Australian legless lizards

Scaly-foot

Tokay gecko

Racerunners and tegus

Jungle runner

Iguanas, agamas, and chameleons

Green iguana

Venomous lizards

Komodo dragon

Old World lizards

Sanddiver

Amphisbaenia

Mexican worm lizard

Cape dwarf chameleon

Sail-tail lizard

American alligator lizard

Mexican beaded lizard

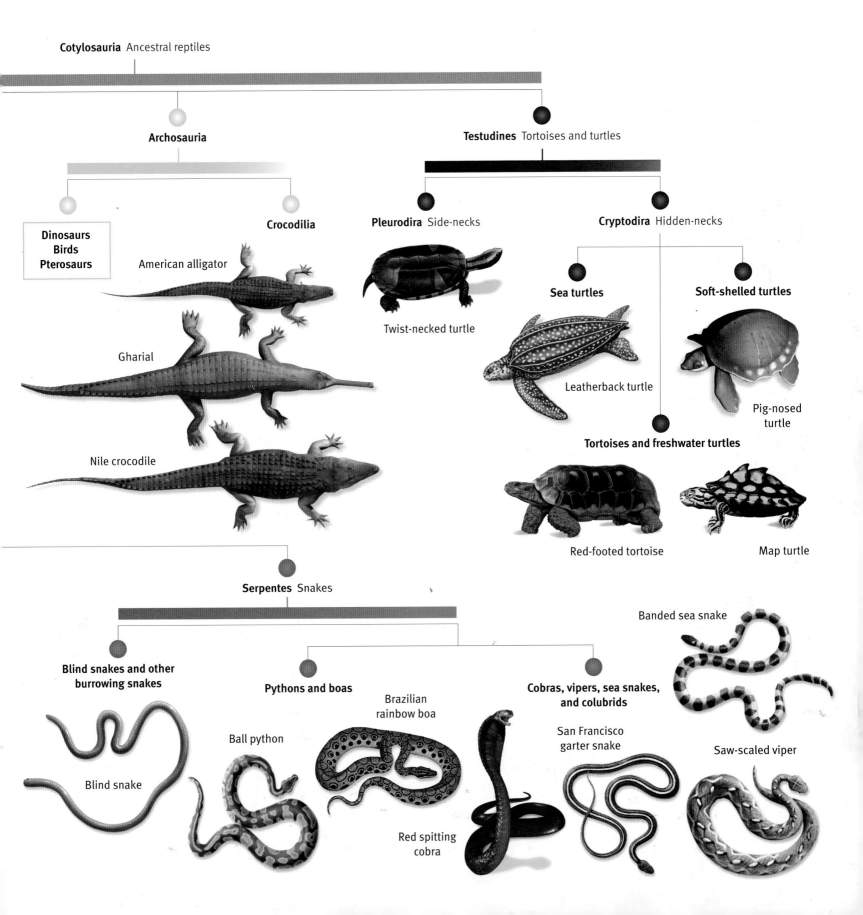

Cotylosauria Ancestral reptiles

Archosauria

Testudines Tortoises and turtles

Crocodilia

Pleurodira Side-necks

Cryptodira Hidden-necks

Dinosaurs
Birds
Pterosaurs

American alligator

Sea turtles

Soft-shelled turtles

Twist-necked turtle

Gharial

Leatherback turtle

Pig-nosed turtle

Nile crocodile

Tortoises and freshwater turtles

Red-footed tortoise

Map turtle

Serpentes Snakes

Banded sea snake

Blind snakes and other burrowing snakes

Pythons and boas

Brazilian rainbow boa

Cobras, vipers, sea snakes, and colubrids

San Francisco garter snake

Ball python

Saw-scaled viper

Blind snake

Red spitting cobra

Glossary

adaptation The way animal species and other living things adjust their features and behavior to survive.

amphibian An animal with a backbone and moist skin, such as a frog or salamander, that can live on land and in water. They lay eggs with jellylike shells.

amphisbaenian A group of specialized legless "worm lizards." They live underground in burrows. Most species have heads similar in shape to their tail and their name means "going both ways."

ancestor A plant or animal from which a later form of plant or animal evolved.

antivenin Medication used to neutralize the poisonous venom in a snakebite.

aquatic Living most or all of the time in water.

arboreal Living in trees or adapted to life in trees.

bask To sit in the sun in order to increase body temperature.

beak A substitute for teeth in turtles and birds. The projecting jaws have a sharp cutting edge made from keratin.

binocular vision The ability to focus both eyes at once on an object. This enables an animal to judge the distance to the object.

brille A clear, fixed scale that covers and protects the eye. It mostly features in animals without eyelids, such as snakes.

camouflage Coloring or body patterns that help an animal blend in with the background.

carapace The upper part of the shell of a turtle or tortoise. The bottom part of the shell is called the plastron.

carnivore An animal that eats meat.

chelonian The general term for all turtles and tortoises.

claws Sharp, curved nails on the toes of animals, which are used to catch prey, dig, and climb.

climate The weather that occurs in a region over a long period of time.

cold-blooded A misleading term that describes an animal, such as a reptile, that cannot warm its body by internal means. It relies on the Sun and warm surfaces to heat its body.

colubrid A diverse group of snakes found around the world; most of the familiar snakes of the Northern Hemisphere belong to this group.

concertina movement A kind of locomotion used by some legless lizards and snakes. The animal moves by stretching part of its body forward in a gripping motion, then pulls the rest along to follow.

crest A row of pointed scales on the back and neck of some lizards.

crocodilian The general term for all crocodiles, alligators, caimans, and gharials.

defense tactics Any behavior an animal uses to escape injury or death by a predator.

desert A dry region with very little rainfall.

dewlap Loose, brightly colored throat skin that a lizard fans out as a signal to other lizards.

dinosaur A group of reptiles that dominated Earth 245–65 million years ago. Dinosaurs are more closely related to crocodilians and birds than to other reptiles.

display A set of behaviors used by animals to communicate with other animals. Displays can send signals to attract potential mates or to frighten rivals or possible predators.

diurnal Active during the day.

egg tooth A special pointed tooth on the tip of the snout of a baby reptile that helps it break through its eggshell when it hatches. The egg tooth falls off soon after hatching.

elapid A family of snakes, such as cobras and sea snakes, with short, fixed fangs at the front of the upper jaw.

elongated Long and thin.

endangered species A species of animal or plant in danger of becoming extinct.

evolution When plants or animals slowly change their characteristics over generations so that they can better adapt to their environment.

extinct No longer living. When the last individual of a species dies, the species is then extinct.

fang A specialized tooth with a groove or canal that enables venom to be injected into prey.

flippers The broad front limbs of sea turtles that are modified to form swimming paddles. Flippers are composed mainly of the bones of the fingers and hand.

fossil The preserved impression of an animal's body or a plant in rock, or evidence of an animal's activity, for example, footprints.

habitat The place where an animal lives in the wild, such as a forest or desert. A habitat provides what the animal needs to survive—food, water, shelter, and mates.

heat pit A pocket within the face scales of certain snakes—such as pythons, boas, and some vipers—that can detect the distance and direction of a source of heat. Snakes use them to find warm-blooded prey in the dark.

herbivore An animal that eats only plants.

hibernate To be asleep or only partly awake during winter. Some lizards and snakes that live in cold climates or in mountain areas hibernate in burrows beneath the snow.

incubate To protect and keep eggs at the right temperature by sitting on them or placing them in nests. This process allows an embryo to develop and hatch.

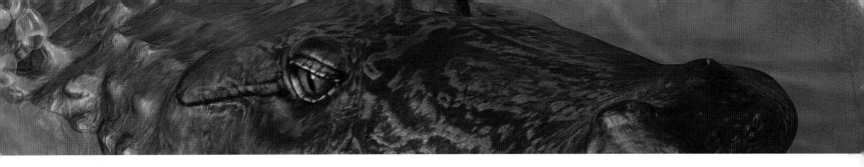

invertebrate An animal that does not have a backbone. They often have a soft body or a hard shell instead.

Jacobson's organ Two small sensory pockets in the roof of the mouth of some lizards and snakes. The tongue transports chemicals in the air, ground, or water to the organ for detection.

keratin A tough material made by skin cells, which forms the outer layer of scales and claws. Human fingernails are made of keratin.

lateral undulation A kind of movement used by some legless lizards and snakes. Curves of the body push back against the rough ground and the animal moves forward through the curved path.

live-bearing Reptiles that do not lay eggs, but give birth to fully formed young.

mammal A group of animals with backbones that have hair or fur. Female mammals feed their young with their own milk.

marine Living in the ocean.

membrane A thin sheet of skin or tissue that lines a part of the body.

mya Million years ago.

nocturnal Active at night.

osteoderm An internal lump or plate of bone in a reptile's skin that provides protection against predators. Most crocodilians and some lizards are protected by osteoderms as well as thick, strong skin.

pigment cells Color-producing cells that determine the skin and eye color in animals.

predator An animal that hunts, kills, and eats other animals.

prey An animal that is hunted, killed, and eaten by other animals.

pupil The round or slit-shaped opening at the front of the eye that lets light enter.

rain forest A thick forest habitat in places where rainfall is very high.

rectilinear locomotion A movement used by large snakes when moving slowly in a straight line. Small sections of the body push backward against the ground while other small sections of the body are pulled forward to new positions.

reptile An air-breathing animal with scaly skin and a backbone. They lay shelled eggs to reproduce. Crocodiles, lizards, snakes, and turtles are all reptiles.

rival An animal that competes with another for food, territory, or a mate.

savanna A flat grassland with thinly spread trees and shrubs. These habitats are found in hot regions, such as Africa.

scales The thickened plates of a reptile's skin that form a protective surface.

scutes The horny plates that cover a chelonian's bony shell and a crocodilian's back.

side-necked A turtle that tucks the head into the shell by bending the neck sideways. Other turtles, called hidden-necked turtles, draw the head vertically back into the shell.

sidewinder movement A form of movement used by some snakes on sand. As the snake anchors its head and tail in the loose sand, it lifts the middle of its body and moves sideways. This means only small sections of its body touch the hot ground at any one time.

species A group of animals that are similar in appearance and share many genetic characteristics. Members of the same species mate and produce offspring.

strike The action of a snake as it suddenly thrusts the head forward to bite.

tail The part of an animal's backbone that extends at the rear. Sometimes, it can move freely.

temperate Regions that have a moderate climate; they are neither very hot nor very cold.

terrestrial Living on land.

territory An area of land inhabited by an animal that may contain its food and its nest. It is common for animals to fiercely defend their territories against intruders.

throat flap A muscular skin flap in the throat of a crocodilian that prevents water from entering its lungs when it is underwater.

tortoise *see* turtle

toxin A poisonous chemical.

trachea A tough tube, called the windpipe, that transfers air from the throat to the lungs.

tropics The regions on either side of the Equator that are warm all year round.

tuatara The name given by the Maori people to a unique New Zealand reptile, similar to a lizard in appearance. There are only two surviving rhynchocephalian species, which is an otherwise extinct group of reptiles.

turtle A reptile with a bony or leathery shell that protects its head, limbs, and tail. There is no strict technical distinction between the words turtle and tortoise.

venom A poisonous liquid injected by some animals, such as snakes, when biting another animal. It is used to disable or kill prey, or in defense against a predator. Antivenin is medicine used to treat people who have been bitten by venomous animals.

vertebra One of the small bones that form the backbone, or spinal column, of an animal.

vertebrate An animal that has an internal skeleton, including a backbone.

warm-blooded An animal, such as a bird or mammal, that produces its own body heat using energy from food.

Index

Credits

The publisher thanks Bronwyn Sweeney and Maria Harding for their contributions, and Jo Rudd for the index.

Key t=top, tl=top left, tc=top center, tr=top right, cl=center left, c=center, cr=center right, bl=bottom left, bcl=bottom center left, bc=bottom center, bcr=bottom center right, br=bottom right

MAPS
Andrew Davies/Creative Communication

ILLUSTRATIONS
Front cover The Art Agency (Mick Posen); **Back cover** The Art Agency (Gary Hanna) tr; (Terry Pastor) c; (Barry Croucher) bl; **Spine** The Art Agency (Gary Hanna); **The Art Agency (Barry Croucher)** 8–9, 10–11, 14–15, 42–3, 44–5, 46–7, 50–1; **(Gary Hanna)** 6–7, 13tr, 18–19, 26–7, 32–3, 38–9, 52–3, 54–5; **(Terry Pastor)** 20–1, 22–3, 28–9, 40–1, 56–7; **(Mick Posen)** 12–13, 24–5, 30–1, 34–5, 36–7, 48–9, 58–9; **(Peter Scott)** 16bl, 60bcr; **Christer Eriksson** 16–17; **Dr David Kirshner** 60bcl, c, bcr, 61tc, bc

PHOTOGRAPHS
AUS=Auscape International, CBT=Corbis, GI=Getty Images, MP=Minden Pictures, NHPA=Natural History Photographic Agency, TPL=photolibrary.com, VU=Visuals Unlimited, WWI=Woodfall/Photoshot

13tc GI; **16**cl WWI; **18**tr NHPA; **22**bl1 CBT; bl2 NHPA; bl3 TPL; bl4 GI; **26**tr CBT; **28**br NHPA; **32**cr GI; **38**cr MP; **39**cr TPL; **40**bl NHPA; **44**br1, br2 GI; **46**bl TPL; **48**t VU; br NHPA; **51**tl TPL; **55**cr CBT; **56**bl TPL; **58**bl1 AUS; bl2, bl3 CBT; bc NHPA

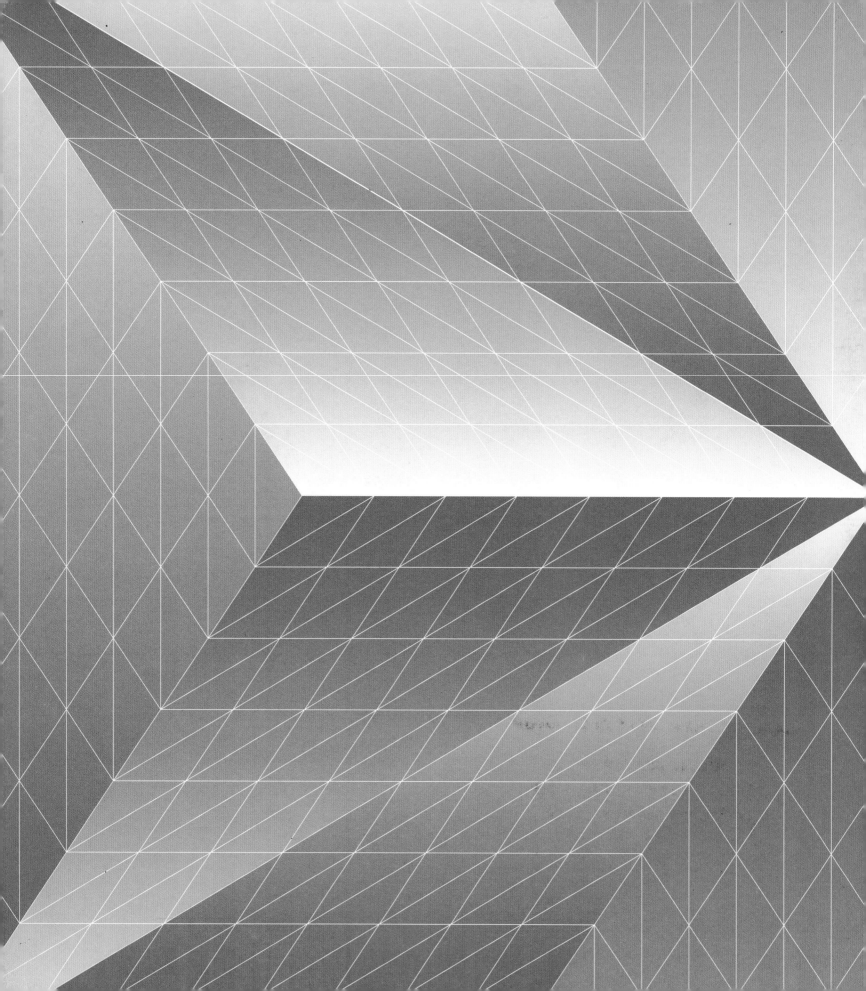